Traditional Inuit Clothing

WRITTEN BY
Nadia Mike

2

For thousands of years, Inuit have used traditional clothing to keep warm during the long winter months. It can get extremely cold in the Arctic, especially in the most northern parts.

4

Traditional clothing was made from different types of skin and fur. The most common animals used were caribou, ringed seals, harp seals, and bearded seals.

After the arrival of Europeans, traditional clothing began to change. Different kinds of fabric, like cotton, were introduced. Inuit began to **incorporate** those materials into their traditional designs. But before this, Inuit depended completely on animals for clothing.

Parkas

Parkas were normally worn by men. Men spent a lot of time outdoors. They hunted throughout the long winters and spent time on the water during the summers. This meant parkas had to be waterproof and able to keep the hunter warm in the harshest weather.

Styles of parkas differed from region to region and were made using a number of different animals.

Parkas were made with two layers so they would be extra warm. The *atigi* is the inner layer, with fur facing in. The *qulittaq* is the outer layer, with fur facing out.

People of all ages still use parkas today. They can now be sewn with a sewing machine. Parkas today can be made from southern fabrics, like commander cloth, and traditional materials, like sealskin. These different materials can be combined to make a parka.

Did You Know?

Children used to wear full-body suits made of caribou skin! These kept their whole bodies warm as they played outside.

Amautiit

An amauti is a style of parka created to carry an infant in a pouch on the back. The hood is larger than the hood of a parka, and it has a long, stylish tail. Amautiit are usually worn by women. The traditional amauti was made using sealskins and caribou skins.

Amautiit are still used today. They are now sewn with a sewing machine using both traditional and new materials. They are decorated with coloured trimmings.

Pants

Pants were made using sealskins and caribou skins. They were made to be lightweight and comfortable. The sealskins, caribou skins, and polar bear skins were **flexible**, so hunters could move easily.

Traditional Inuit pants were as functional and practical as the parka. Today, pants are still made of skins from seals, caribou, and polar bears. Sometimes they are filled with eider-duck down or muskox hair.

Pants can also be made of a polyester and cotton blend with an **insulated** lining.

Mitts

Mitts protected the hands from the freezing Arctic. They were usually made from sealskins or caribou skins, but they could also be made using other types of animal skins. Women's and men's mitts used the same pattern but varied in size.

Today, mitts can be made from different materials, like leather or sheep's wool. Of course, skins from seals, caribou, wolves, and beavers still make the warmest mitts.

Kamiit

Kamiit are traditional Inuit footwear. They are normally made of caribou skins and sealskins, with soles made of bearded sealskins.

Traditionally, kamiit were sewn using caribou and narwhal **sinew**. Sinew swells when it is wet, which closes up the holes created by sewing needles. Stitches then become waterproof.

Like pants and parkas, kamiit also have a number of layers to them. Usually duffle socks and slippers are worn inside the outer layer of the kamiit.

Kamiit are very beautiful. Today, duffle socks are decorated with **embroidered** details.

Conclusion

Today, Inuit of all ages wear a mix of traditional and modern clothing. New materials are sometimes used, but animal skins are still very important for getting through the harsh Arctic winters.

Traditional Inuit clothing is made to be warm and functional. But it is also meant to be beautiful. Parkas, amautiit, pants, mitts, and kamiit can be works of art!

Glossary

embroidered
decorated with a needle and thread.

flexible
easily able to stretch and move.

incorporate
to combine different things, for example,
something new with something old.

insulated
made to stop heat or cold from passing
through.

sinew
a tough material that connects muscle
to bone.